LANDFORMS

by Kelli Hicks

Published in the United States of America by Cherry Lake Publishing Group
Ann Arbor, Michigan
www.cherrylakepublishing.com

Reading Adviser: Beth Walker Gambro, MS, Ed., Reading Consultant, Yorkville, IL

Photo Credits:
© Nicoleta Ionescu/Shutterstock, (cartoon boy on cover and throughout book), © JimmyMore/Shutterstock, (photo) cover; © Cassette Bleue/Shutterstock, speech bubbles throughout; © ORION PRODUCTION/Shutterstock, (top), © AlviseZiche/Shutterstock, page 5; © BlueRingMedia/Shutterstock, (illustration), © Viacheslav Lopatin/Shutterstock, , (Earth), page 7; © Manuela Durson/Shutterstock, (top), © Attapol Yiemsiriwut/Shutterstock, page 8; © Brent Coulter/Shutterstock, (top), © CHAOSPHERE/Shutterstock, (plate movements), © Zaporizhzhia vector/Shutterstock, (map), page 9; © Daniel Prudek/Shutterstock, (top), © Ko Zatu/Shutterstock, page 10; © dragana serbia/Shutterstock, (top), © Todd Boland/Shutterstock, page 11; © Leonid Andronov/Shutterstock, (top), © Alexey Suloev/Shutterstock, page 12; © Nomad Pixel/Shutterstock, (top), © S B Stock/Shutterstock, © CHAOSPHERE/Shutterstock, illustrations, page 13; © Sabbir Digital/Shutterstock, (large photo), pages 14-15; ©Lubo Ivanko/Shutterstock, (top), page 14; © Mozgova/Shutterstock, (top), page 15; © Porstocker/Shutterstock, (globe), page 16, © FiledIMAGE/Shutterstock, (top), © Freelancer Anab/Shutterstock, page 17; © Tomas Kulaja/Shutterstock, (small photo), page 18, © Sergey Dudikov/Shutterstock, (large photo), pages 18-19; © naokita/Shutterstock, (top), © Tracy Burroughs Brown/Shutterstock, page 19; © Skreidzeleu/Shutterstock, pages 20-21

Produced by bluedooreducation.com for Cherry Lake Publishing

Copyright © 2026 by Cherry Lake Publishing Group

All rights reserved. No part of this book may be reproduced or utilized in any form or by any means without written permission from the publisher.

Library of Congress Cataloging-in-Publication Data has been filed and is available at catalog.loc.gov.

Printed in the United States of America

Note from Publisher: Websites change regularly, and their future contents are outside of our control. Supervise children when conducting any recommended online searches for extended learning opportunities.

TABLE OF CONTENTS

Many Kinds of Landforms 4

Moving Earth 8

Up and Down 10

Staying Dry 14

Wet Landforms 16

Think About It 22

Glossary 23

Find Out More 24

Index 24

About the Author 24

MANY KINDS OF LANDFORMS

Look at the cover of this book.
What does it show?

A canyon is a deep, narrow valley. A canyon is made by water wearing away rock.

It takes millions of years for water to form a canyon.

Some canyons no longer have water.

5

Canyons, mountains, hills, valleys, oceans, and rivers are all **landforms**.

Landforms give shape to the earth. They provide homes for plants and animals.

hills

ocean

MOVING EARTH

Wind and water cause soil and rocks to move into different places.

8

When soil and rocks move, the shape of the land changes.

Did You Know?

Under Earth's **surface** are giant slabs of rock, called tectonic plates. When they move, they cause the land to shift. The plates can push against each other or move away from each other. Movement of the plates can cause earthquakes, or cause volcanoes to **erupt**.

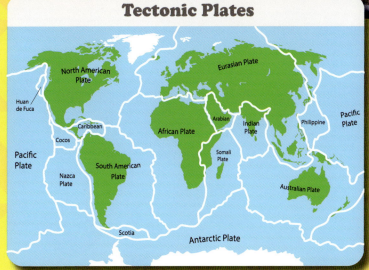

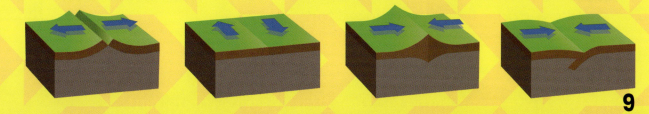

9

UP AND DOWN

Some landforms, such as mountains, rise up from the surface of the earth. Mountains are the tallest landforms.

Mount Everest is part of the Himalayan Mountain Range. It is the tallest mountain in the world.

1 Rises up from Earth's surface

2 Has a pointed top

3 Has **steep** sides

These are some of the features that describe mountains.

Hills and **plateaus** also rise from Earth's surface.

Hills look like small mountains but have rounded tops.

Plateaus have flat tops and rocky sides called cliffs.

hills

plateau

cliff

plateau: plaa-TOH

11

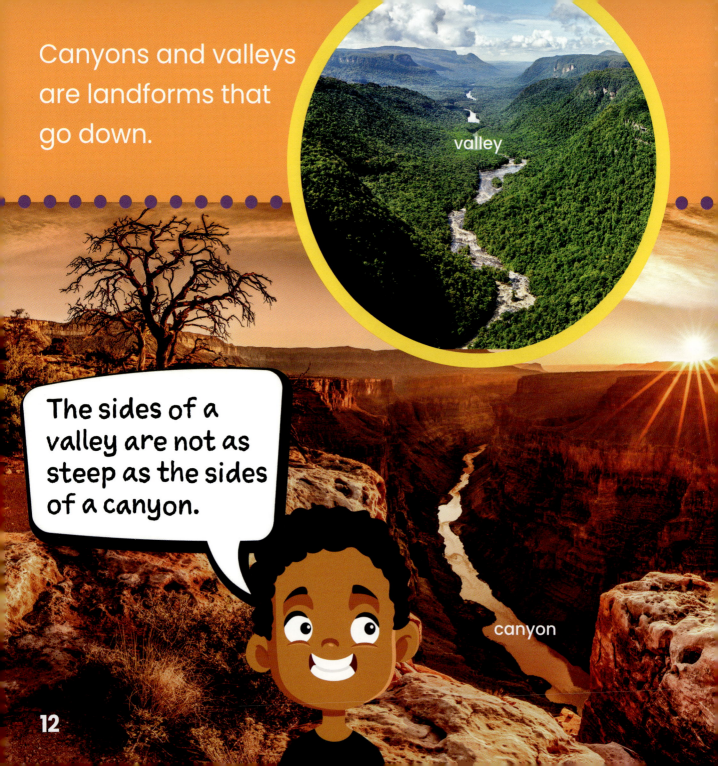

canyon

Fun Fact!

Canyons and valleys can have a U shape or a V shape. U-shaped canyons form from melting **glaciers**. Rivers cause V-shaped canyons.

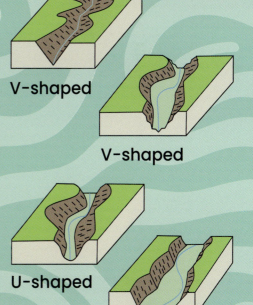

V-shaped

V-shaped

U-shaped

U-shaped

STAYING DRY

A desert is a landform that gets little to no rain. It has few trees and lots of wind. Deserts can be hot or cold.

The Sahara desert in Africa is a hot desert.

WET LANDFORMS

Oceans cover 71% of Earth. Ocean **currents** and waves can change landforms.

An ocean's powerful waves wash away sand and rock.

1 Cover 71% of the Earth

2 Made up of saltwater

3 Home to about a quarter million different kinds of animals

These are some of the features that describe oceans.

17

Freshwater landforms flow into oceans. Lakes, rivers, and creeks move water and help to shape the land.

Rivers run all the way to the oceans.

Landforms change the surface of Earth. Changes can happen slowly or quickly.

The Grand Canyon

Wind, rain, and the Colorado River took millions of years to form the Grand Canyon.

The famous Grand Canyon in Arizona is about 1 mile deep (1.6 kilometers). I get woozy looking down!

THINK ABOUT IT

Using what you have learned in this book, match each sentence to the correct picture.

1 This landform gets little rain.

2 This landform has a deep, narrow valley.

3 This landform has fresh water.

4 This is the tallest of all landforms.

A. mountain

B. lake

C. desert

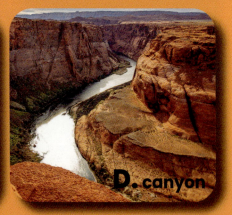
D. canyon

Answers: 1C 2D 3B 4A

GLOSSARY

currents (KUR-uhnts) the movements of water in a river or an ocean

erupt (ih-RUHPT) lava, hot ash, and rocks thrown with great force

glaciers (GLAY-shurz) large, slow-moving masses of ice found in mountain valleys or polar areas

landforms (LAND-formz) natural features of land

plateaus (plaa-TOHZ) areas of high, flat lands

steep (STEEP) sharply sloping up or down

surface (SUR-fiss) the outside or outermost layer of something

FIND OUT MORE

Books

Brennan, Linda Crotta. *U.S. Landforms: What You Need to Know,* Mankato, MN: Capstone Publishing: 2017

Haskell, J.P. *Earth's Many Landforms,* New York, NY: The Rosen Publishing Group: 2017

Websites

Search these online sources with an adult:

Landforms | Britannica

Landforms | Kiddle

INDEX

canyon(s) 4, 5, 6, 12, 13, 21
desert(s) 14, 15
mountain(s) 6, 10, 11
ocean(s) 6, 16, 17, 18

surface 9, 10, 20
water 5, 8, 18
wind 8, 14, 21

ABOUT THE AUTHOR

Kelli Hicks is a teacher, mom, and writer who lives in Tampa, Florida. She loves learning new words and is excited about how many new ideas she can learn while studying science. She can often be found eating chocolate, walking her dog, drinking tea with her daughter, or watching her son play volleyball.